The Limi

Or, Why Should Sceptics Be Outlaws?

George Jacob Holyoake

Alpha Editions

This edition published in 2022

ISBN : 9789356891579

Design and Setting By
Alpha Editions
www.alphaedis.com
Email - info@alphaedis.com

PREFACE.

The object of these pages* is not to defend the intellectual accuracy of Atheism (which could not be attempted in this brief space), the object is to explain its case, to vindicate its moral rectitude, and the right of those who hold these views, to legal equality. There are two Atheisms in literature—the ancient one of mere negation; and the affirmative form, whose relevant name is Cosmism, and of which Humboldt, in his 'Cosmos,' is a great illustrator, and Comte, in his 'Positive Philosophy,' an expounder. The term Cosmism ought to supersede the misleading term Atheism; just as Secularism has superseded the libellous term Infidelity. Cosmism, as well as Secularism, expresses a new form of Freethought, and I use the term Atheism, as the subject of a Lecture, for the first time here. It is a worn-out word, used by Theists in hateful senses. I employ it, as a title, to-day for political reasons, in order to show those who make it a ground of civil exclusion, that it is a thing of law and limits: that the reputed Atheism of English working men, so far as it prevails, is no longer the old Atheism of mere negation, but the Cosmism of modern science; neither dissolute, anarchical, nor impious—recognises that the universe is, without theorising *why* it is. Negative Atheism says there is nothing beyond the universe. Cosmism says it cannot explain anything beyond, and pauses where its knowledge ends.

**A report of a Lecture delivered in Bendall's Assembly Rooms, City Road, London, March 8rd, 1861.*

Atheism questions—Cosmism affirms. The language of Cosmism is that of the poet in the 'Purgatory of Suicides':—

'I do not say—there is no God,
But this I say—I know not.'

I prefer Secularism, which concerns itself with the moral life of man, and maintains a well-advised neutrality upon these speculative questions. My sympathies are with 'Adam Bede,' that striking and greatest creation of modern genius, in which the *National Review* recognised 'The strong-headed, manly, sharp-tempered, secular carpenter, with his energetic satisfaction in his work, and impatience of dreamers.' But as I stated in the York Debate, in 1858, at which the Reverend Canons Hey and Robinson presided, it is an act of self-defence in England to question the assumed infallibility of Theism—to prove that Atheists are entitled to civil recognition, as persons having legitimate, actual, and conscientious views, and who, therefore, ought not to be outlawed as they are now. So long as sceptics of Theism are refused the right of affirmation in courts of law, and their lives and property consequently placed at the mercy of every ruffian and knave, so long will a Sceptical propaganda be a parliamentary necessity, to justify these opinions, and to spread them, that those who hold them may, like the Quakers, win by pertinacity what is denied to reason. And while this state of things lasts, I confess that I listen to arguments of opponents with distrust, for I see in them, not so much the confutation of my opinions, as the limitation of my freedom, and the justification of my political exclusion. In the present state of theological liberty in England, for the alleged Atheist to be silent, is to be a slave consenting to his own degradation.

G. J. H.

147, Fleet Street, London, E.C., April 13th, 1861.

THE LIMITS OF ATHEISM

Twenty years ago I stepped forward to defend the right of expressing Atheism on the part of those who conscientiously held it. On Mr. Southwell's imprisonment in Bristol, I took his place as Editor of the *Oracle of Reason*, and shared his fate at Gloucester. Under the same circumstances I would do it again to-morrow. In the expression of speculative opinions there may be error and there may be outrage; but the error is best corrected by discussion, and the outrage by cultivation; but to prohibit the free publication of opinion is to strike at the root of all intrepidity of thought and individuality of character; and against a uniformity of profession, whether brought about by the tyranny of the majority, by the policeman, or by the magistrate, I ever have, and ever will, protest as unwise, dishonest, and degrading.

Because Atheistical opinions were attacked by the law I defended them: I defended the right to hold them without sharing them. And in all the publications I have edited, I have accepted the responsibility of the views of coadjutors and correspondents without conditions, and my name is associated in consequence much more with other persons' opinions than with my own. When the rights of conscience in Free-thought are attacked, to discriminate is to condemn; and while persecution is attempted, I make it a point of honour never to pass in appearance on to the side of the persecutors. As soon as legal opposition to the publication of heretical opinion ceased, I was the first to insist that the day of good taste must commence. The moment fair play is permitted, all excuse for invective or outrage ends. Violence, exaggeration, denunciation, are crimes against Freethought the moment Freethought is permitted. Now that Sir George Cornewall Lewis, on the part of the Government, has refused Sir John Trelawny's request to alter the law which treats an Atheist as an outlaw, which denies him the common right of legal protection, which exposes him to plunder or assault without redress, which cedes to the Theist a monopoly of veracity in courts of law, and places the word of every man and woman, however honest, cultivated, and reputable, unable to make a Profession of Faith, as below that of a convicted felon, I am most reluctant to enter upon any explanation of my own views on the great speculative propositions of theology, lest it should appear to others as timidity, retreat, or disposition to compromise.. If a man had (which I have not) a change of opinion to own, this is not the hour to make it. But with respect to Affirmative Atheism, the necessity for newness of view is chiefly felt by those who do not understand it. It is refused civil recognition because it is conceived to be some lawless thing. The consternation excited just now by the 'Essays and Reviews' is owing to an apprehension that public opinion is tending to the negation of theology, and that is concluded to be a state of intellectual lawlessness. To trace any outline of the Limits of Atheism, may serve to give more intelligent definiteness to the misgivings entertained concerning it, and lead earlier to its legal recognition; and therefore alone I attempt it.

Let us avoid verbiage if we can. Too many words are the locusts of the mind, which darken the air of the understanding and eat up our meaning. I believe that language is given us not to be used—except upon clear compulsion.

There are two terms which especially excite religious reprobation, and one of them excites mine. I refer to Infidelity and Atheism.

Infidelity is a term I detest. It implies that you believe enough to subject you to reproach, and disbelieve enough to entitle you to be damned. It signifies disbelief too inveterate to allow you to go back to superstition, and too much timidity to carry your doubt to a definite or legitimate result. I am for thoroughness and decision. If it be criminality to disbelieve, I will put scepticism far from me. I will not even tamper with doubt. But if it be lawful to reject from the understanding whatever seems false, then I will disbelieve error as a duty, and unhesitatingly doubt whatever is doubtful.

Atheism—objectionable as it is from wanton negative associations—is a far more wholesome term. It is a defiant, militant word. There is a ring of decision about it. There is no cringing in it. It keeps no terms with superstition. It makes war, and means it. It carries you away from the noisome word-jugglery of the conventional pulpits, and brings you face to face with nature. It is a relief to get out of the crowd who believe because their neighbours do, who pray by rote, and worship through fear; and win your liberty to wander in the refreshing solitude where the heart may be honest, and the intellect free. Affirmative Atheism of the intellect is a proud, honest, intrepid, self-respecting attitude of the mind. The Negative Atheism of mere ignorance, of insensibility, of lust, and gluttony, and drunkenness, of egotism or vanity, whose talk is outrage, and whose spirit is blasphemy; this is the gross negation of God, which superstition begets in its slavery, and nurtures by its terrors. These species of Atheism I recognise only to disown and denounce them. Of these the priest is the author who preaches the natural corruption of the human heart, who inculcates the guilt of Freethought, the distrust of reason, and despair of self-reliant progress. Utterly different from this is the Atheism of reflection, which seeks for conclusive evidence, which listens reverentially for the voice of God, which weighs carefully the teachings of a thoughtful Theism; but refuses to recognise the officious, incoherent babblement of intolerant or presumptuous men. Reflective Atheism is simply a reluctant uncertainty as to the consciousness of Nature, or as to the existence of a Power over Nature. As one who will allow me the pleasure of calling him my friend, Mr. G. H. Lewes, said, all reflective Atheism is suspensive.

He invented the phrase Suspensive Atheism to describe the only form of opinion which he knew I maintained. The thoughtful Atheist wishes to perceive the whole truth of Nature, he hesitates unwillingly, and waits longingly for more light.

Let us dismiss at once that crude and evasive state which affects Atheism, and, at the same time, denies it; which says no Theist has defined Deity, and therefore the disbelief in it is an impossibility.

Affirmative Atheism may be wrong, but it is at least intelligible. It has a definite foundation, or it could claim no position, and would deserve none. It must go upon facts if it would maintain a place in the kingdom of thought, and it finds these facts in Positivism. The mind that has wandered in the torrid zones of error, thirsts ardently for the cooling draughts of positive truth. It is this sentiment which causes Freethought to take the form of Secularism, and exchanges the verbal distractions of conflicting creeds for the clear criterions of moral truth. It is the same wise impatience of metaphysical unrealities which leads to Affirmative Atheism, and explains it. A series of material and mental facts arrest the attention of one taking an unbiased and independent view of the universe, of time, and space, and matter.

There are two classes of thinkers—one who commence with ignoring Nature, seeking in something outside it for the origin of it, and who look upon the infinite processes of the worlds which people space, with the dull astonishment accorded to mere agencies, rather than with the native wonder and awe which the consciousness of original powers awakens—these are Theists.

The other class are those who regard matter as the very garment of the unknown God, to whom every spray, and pebble, and flower, and star is a marvel, a glory, and an inspiration; who, comprehending not an external cause of nature, recognise its existence, its surpassing affluence, its multitudinous marvels, and give them the first place in their wonder, study, reverence, and love—these are Affirmative Atheists.

To believe in Nature, in its self-existence, its self-subsistence, its self-action, its eternity, infinity, and materiality, and in that only, is Affirmative Atheism.* Reflective Atheism is pure inability to, realise the fact of the consciousness of the universe, or to conceive the existence of a Being over it.

To believe in something besides nature—is Theism.

To believe in the consciousness of nature—is Pantheism.

The explanation of Affirmative Atheism* here given, involves many considerations which I am not going to discuss. It is not my province here to defend, but to state the case. A definition is a map, but it is not the journey. A definition is a high road through a subject, and a high road should be a straight road: it may run out of the way of some populous towns and beautiful scenes, but it gives the means of quickest transit through a territory, from which the country can be viewed, and the traveller determine its general features.

** This might stand for a definition of Cosmism, which term I employ at substantially reciprocal with Affirmative Atheism, and as its substitute, if I may employ it in its modern and wider sense than defined by Pythagoras.*

If we have said enough for this purpose, we may attempt to trace the limits of our subject. The road through every high question lies over precipices. Every great question has its Mont Blancs. The higher you climb the deeper the chasms on the right hand and on the left. The Roman Catholic makes worship an art, and abject submission a duty. To relieve you of anxiety he deprives the mind of initiation and freedom. The Protestant concedes you private judgment, and surrounds you by a social despotism lest you should use it. He substitutes a creed for the Church. The Church is a cell, and the creed is a cage. The cage is lighter, more airy, and less repulsive than the cell, but the imprisonment is complete in both.

Mere Atheism inculcates freedom and intrepidity of the understanding, but may land you in negation, in dogmatism, in denunciation, in irreverence. These are the chasms that lie in the path of mere Atheism. The traveller who passes into these is lost. To avoid this danger we must keep within the limits naturally prescribed to Affirmative Atheism, which are:—

1. Positivism in Principle.

2. Exactness in Profession of Opinion.

3. Dispassionateness in Judgment.

4. Humanism in Conception.

1. The Positivist conception of Atheism exhibits the limits which modern thought has impressed upon it. Affirmative Atheism asserts the realism of Nature; Theism denies it. Theism refuses to recognise the self-existence, the self-action, the self-subsistence, eternity, and infinity of the universe. Theism is the negation of Nature. It is a species of impiety towards nature, and supplants, by an artificial superstition, the instinctive reverence of the human heart.

Modern Atheism is falsely regarded as a mere negation, as a species of criminal vacuity of the understanding. To correct this idea is to win for these opinions attention if not assent. The negation of any error is useful, but it should be followed by its complement of positive truth. All mere negative subjects are like the lime and pebbles swallowed by farm fowl to assist digestion, but it fares ill with the fowl if they get nothing but stones to digest; if no corn or barley follows to be operated upon. Now, questions of Atheism and Scepticism are the digestive stimuli of the mind; positive principles supply the corn and barley which sustain the mental system and preserve its life. If we give ourselves up to negative subjects merely, we come to resemble the theologians who, as Talleyrand said, 'pick a great many bones for very little meat.'

Old Atheism shows that the alleged proofs of the existence of a Deity are inconclusive, untenable, or self-refutatory. As a discipline of the intellect, as a questioning of that theistical speculation which has always been arrogant and tyrannical towards dissentients, there is good in negative Atheism. But it is more important if made to subserve practical objects. Mere negative Atheism has no ulterior objects it untenants the mind, and this may not be in all things beneficial. The slave may be more healthy who is forced to take exercise, and he may have more physical enjoyment of life than the indolent freeman, who is sedentary by choice, and diseased through inactivity and overfeeding.

You may pluck up weeds, and the rank herbage be more fruitful of miasma than the weeds; or if the plucked up weeds produce no harm, the ground may be left useless until crops are made to grow upon it. So of the weeds of worship which spring up in the priest-ridden mind. Reverence may be cultivated by superstition, good conduct maybe enforced by terror; if superstition and terror be exploded, the reverence and good conduct must be cared for and be better directed. Freethought is no half work, it has much to do.

It is delusive to pull down the altar of superstition and not erect an altar of science in its place. To pack up the household gods of superstition and leave the fireside bare, will hardly do.. Affirmative Atheism must teach that nature is the Bible of truth, work is worship, that duty is dignity, and the unselfish service of others consolation.

There is nothing wholly bad. Superstition has in it some elements of good. I no more believe in perfect error than in perfect truth. Error, like truth, is hardly ever found pure; error is mixed with good, and truth alloyed by evil. The mind must have something to feed upon, and if it cannot have truth, it will have superstition; and though superstition, like some diet, is very hard of digestion, and very innutritious, it is better to feed upon that than die. True, it keeps the mind thin, but it keeps it alive, and it is better to be a skeleton than a corpse. Now it is true that some intellects, like some animals, eat by instinct the right kind of food, but being healthy are not fastidious, and if you give them bad food they don't object to it and don't care for it. If they take it, their digestion is so good that it does not hurt them. But there are other people who pine for the knowledge of nature, and cannot subsist unless a large proportion of their mental aliment consists of definite principle. When these are not supplied by religious teachers, and Christianity by any intolerance prevents it being supplied by others, such natures expire in an intellectual sense, and Christianity ought to be regarded as guilty of wilful murder. And in the case of Atheism, those persons who are accustomed to take superstition, and are deprived of that, and no attempt is made to supply its place by more wholesome sustenance, are no doubt injured. Negative Atheism guilty of this neglect may be said to be guilty of manslaughter, and it would be murder were the neglect accompanied, as in the case of Theism, by intolerance. Beware of reckless iconoclasticism.

Mere negations give all advantage to superstition; error seems wisdom and wealth when truth is silent.

2. The logic of Affirmative Atheism begins in self-confession. Not to see anything where there is nothing to be seen is the sign of the true faculty; and not to say that you do see when you do not is the first sign of veracity of intellect.

Man is forgiven who believes more than his neighbours, but he is never forgiven if he believes less. If he believes more than his neighbours, there is the presumption that he may have made some discovery which may become profitable one day to join in. It may be that he who believes most, may merely possess a more industrious credulity, or possess a greater capacity for hasty assumption. But this is seldom probed. He who believes less may have abandoned some important item of justifiable belief. But when he who believes less than the multitude, confesses to the fact in the face of public disapproval, the probability is that he has inquired into, and sifted evidence which others have taken for granted, and discovered some error which they have accepted. His greater accuracy of mind and exactness of speech are an offence, because a reproach to the careless or unscrupulous intellects of those who conduct life on secondhand opinions. Yet austerity of intellect and austerity of speech is as wholesome in character, as austerity of morals. I hope, says Mr. Grote, in his great history of Greece, in a memorable passage that ought not to die out of recollection, 'I hope, when I come to the lives of Socrates and Plato, to illustrate one of the most valuable of their principles, that conscious and confessed ignorance is a better state of mind than the fancy without the reality of knowledge.' And in a passage which I cannot now recall, Lord Brougham has said that 'a mind uninformed is better than a mind misinformed.' In a state of ignorance we do nothing, in a state of error we do wrong. The popular condemnation of the Atheist—which we have lately heard as ignorantly echoed in the House of Commons as in some Conventicles—is not always uttered, because the Atheist does not know more than others, for none know anything certain concerning the existence of God,* but because the Atheist does not profess more.

** In his remarkable work entitled 'First Principles,' now in course of publication, Mr. Herbert Spencer has shown that certain terms of Cosmism are as incapable of ultimate explanation as certain terms of Theism. This shows how unwise is dogmatism, how unjustifiable is intolerance, on either side.*

Cosmism, a thoughtful name, which ought to supersede Atheism in the future, neither denies nor affirms the existence of Deity. It waits for explanation and proof. It admits there is evidence of something, but what that something is, does not appear. There is evidence of more than we know, but what that is we do not know, and it is dishonesty to use a term respecting it, which pretends that we do know. Why should it not be honourable to observe a scientific reservation in the exposition of opinion? In science it is a sign of cultivation to understate a case and keep within the limits of fact and proof. The reservation of Cosmism, which so many regard as an offence, arises from a love of exact truth, from an endeavour to attain to it in expression, and from an honourable unwillingness to employ words which do not represent to him who uses them, definite ideas.

If we say God is Light, Love, Truth, Power, Goodness, Law, Principle, we confound attributes with existence. If we say God is a Spirit, God is space, we merely fill the imagination, not satisfy the understanding: it is feeding the thoughts with air, and leaving the intellect hungry. A Trinitarian Deity is one of the scholastic perplexities of the intellect. The first rule of arithmetic is against it. If it means three Gods in one, it is an enigma. If it means three doctrinal aspects of God, it confuses all simplicity of feeling. In the simple, moral heart of man, God is one, and his name is Love; not a weak, vapoury sentimentality, but an austere, healthy love, whose expression is strength, purity, truth, justice, service, and tenderness. But this conception of Deity belongs to the empire of the emotions, it is a matter of feeling, not of proof, and can authorise no intolerance towards others, itself existing only by the sufferance of the intellect, which has chastened its expression, and is supreme over it.

Exactness of phraseology is well understood self-defence. Well chosen terms are the true weapons of opinion. Employing an old, battered, rheumatic and abused term like Atheism, is like riflemen using the old musket instead of the far-reaching and fatal Minie. Cosmism is the new term which conveys the new idea of the age, and explains the improvements in thought and spirit, which the mere term Atheism conceals. To suffer an opponent to choose names for you is as though a combatant should suffer his enemy to supply his arms for the conflict. He who consents to be called by a hateful name, can be defeated at the pleasure of his opponent. His ideas are never discussed, his conscientious spirit is never recognised, he is trampled down by a name which libels, defames, and destroys him. Let us banish the unqualified term Atheism from the literature of theological controversy.

3. Dispassionateness is a law of Affirmative Atheism. Those who commence by believing themselves infallible, and their view of a question open to no dispute, can never see reason in, nor view with patience the dissent which others maintain. It is the first instinct of the Cosmist (to use the preferable term) to keep his mind open to reason. The dogmatism which insists on its own case, and shuts its eyes and closes its ears to the facts and arguments on the side of Theism, is always to be condemned. Dogmatism, the sin of superstition, is excluded from the empire of speculation. The clergyman will often admit that Atheism endeavours to maintain an unprejudiced tone of mind. The Rev. Charles Marriot, of Oriel College, observed to me, when I had the honour some years ago to be his guest, that 'he had always more hope of the Atheist than of the Dissenter, for the Dissenter always moved in a little infallibility of his own, while the Atheist was always to be reached by reason.' Mystery will always conquer partisans, and the Cosmist who comprehends this, will reason with superstition, and never be impatient with it.

Dispassionateness of judgment will also lead to dispassionateness of speech. Opinion in a minority should never have recourse to invective. Prejudice is inveterate enough without being inflamed by denunciation. Unpopular and unfriended truth must consent to placate opposition by respectfulness of tone and fairness of speech. It must never compromise principle—that is submission, and gives the errorist insolent confidence. It must never outrage—that makes the errorist indignant, and deaf to all reason. The force of truth lies in invincible patience and in invincible perseverance of exposition. Progressive opinion ought ever to be kept on the high places of dispassionate advocacy. It is wonderful how truth has been perilled by passion. The battle of opinion has always been fought on impulse, rather than on calculation of forces; and the small band of the combatants for new truths has often been trampled down by the multitudinous army of error.

4. Conceptions of Humanity, or, in other words, Reliance of Humanity, is a law and limit of Affirmative Atheism. Every man who thinks, must choose one of two things, a standard without the universe, or a standard within. I choose one within, I choose humanity. 'Men,' says Lord Bacon, speaking of Atheism, 'who look no farther, become wary of themselves.' Let us become wary of ourselves; nothing is more wholesome or progressive!

Hardness, assumption, egotism, insubordination to worth—in one word, irreverence, ought never to be the characteristic of Cosmism. He who vindicates nature and reason, should show that being left to nature, philosophy, reputation, and the laws, there exists self-regulation and reliable rationality.* Cosmism is the highest form of self-reliance; the responsibility, which to others is a necessity, is to him a duty and a pride.

** As the late Gen. Jacob, the illustrious commander of the Scinde Horse, testifies. 'In the jangle and desert, amid a barbarous people on the extreme confines of civilisation,' he applied these principles when Bishops despaired and Christianity failed; and he records that 'He was permitted to witness with delight the fact of a whole nation being raised from a state of barbarous violence, misery, detestable cruelty, and horror, to one of peace, comfort, racial order, and happiness;' that 'He had seen their faithful and steady application in practice change thousands of the wildest robbers and murderers into kindly and industrious citizens.*

The wildness, excesses, extravagances, and incoherences of superstition, arise through men looking without themselves into those regions of the unknown where men make God after their own image, where they imagine their facts, and reason upon them without check. How impertinent is half our modern worship, and how poor the other half! Educated ministers speak of God, and address to him praise they would be ashamed to offer to any gentleman. That delicacy of reverence, that reticence of laudation, that avoidance of presumption and familiarity, which the law of humanity imposes on all men of religious habits in human relations, has no existence in theology, where it is more to be expected and infinitely more needful. When St. Augustine speaks of God, there is a magnificent thoughtfulness in the terms he employs which his Pagan refinement had taught him, which we seldom find in modern saints. How imposingly he exclaims in his Confessions:—

What art Thou then, my God? Most highest, most good, most potent, most omnipotent; most merciful, yet most just; most hidden, yet most present; most beautiful, yet most strong; stable, yet incomprehensible; unchangeable, yet all-changing; never new, never old; all-renewing, and *bringing age upon the proud, and they know it not*; ever working, ever at rest; still gathering, yet nothing lacking; supporting, filling, and overspreading; creating, nourishing, and maturing; seeking, yet having all things. Thou lovest, without passion; art jealous, without anxiety; repentest, yet grievest not; art angry, yet serene; changest Thy works, Thy purpose unchanged; receivest again what Thou findest, yet didst never lose; never in need, yet rejoicing in gains; never covetous, yet exacting usury. Thou receivest over and above, that Thou mayest owe; and who hath aught that is not Thine? Thou payest debts, owing nothing; remittest debts, losing nothing.'

We forgive the sublime contradictions in the stately march of this Pagan praise. Augustine was a noble old saint, but he had a Pagan intellect to the end.

The 'Limits of Atheism' which obviously present themselves to those who reflect upon them, rescue it from the imputation of lawlessness. Positivism engrafts upon it practical aims. Exactness of speech necessitates exactness of thought, and dictates modesty of pretension. Dispassionateness of judgment checks invective, dogmatism, prejudice, or unfairness; and Reliance upon Humanity tends to self-trust, self-direction, and chastity of worship. Why should persons who hold the views of Affirmative Atheism under these 'Limits' be treated in the witness-box as public liars—men whose reiterated profession is—that they 'sum up personal duty in Honour, which is respecting the Truth; in Morality, which is acting the Truth; and in Love, which is serving the Truth.'*

* *'Last Trial for Atheism,' p. 100.*

Plato in his 'Laws,' remarks that 'Atheism is a disease of the soul before it becomes an error of the understanding.' This just opinion, if applied to mere sensualists, who disbelieve in God because his holiness is a restraint upon their infamous passions, has since been applied to the pure thinkers like Spinoza, to whom it is an insult and an outrage. Let us see how little such a remark is applicable to those who thoughtfully pause before adopting a creed which, however dictated by a feeling of piety, is far less reverential than thoughtful silence.

If we suppose an interposing Providence to direct the affairs of this world, what scenes of sorrow must meet his eye? Condemned to poverty and pain, how many human beings are there whose every word is a prayer, and every thought a throb, and every pulsation a pang? Is it not far more reverential to struggle for the right with what powers we have, and with what Secular light is vouchsafed, and own Theism inscrutable, than connect all this misery with the name of God? The theory of a God of Prayer who hears and aids, of a Providence who orders and controls, all issues to one great Will, and who receives at last the sorrow-stricken, the worn, struggling and weary spirit, after those conflicts which all who think, and feel, and aspire, encounter, are primitive and enduring conceptions, which all humanity, in every age and in every slime, cherishes in its perplexity and clings to in its weakness. It is not Cosmism which seeks or wishes to disprove this theory. Alas! the God of Prayer does not exist. I say it not in wantonness, or recklessness, nor in any proud spirit of defiance, nor in any hard spirit of denial, nor in outrage, nor wilful scepticism, nor simulated disbelief. It appears to me an austere fact, which all who observe must see, which all who are frank must own. Yet I know not that I ought to say 'Alas it is so.' Why should any man mourn at truth? What right have I to arraign the facts of Nature. To mourn what *is*—is to condemn what is. Sorrow is censure when it relates to what is possibly the order of God. What authority have I to look on Nature awful in its glories and mysteries, and by the implication included in my grief, to judge it and say it is not what it should be? My scrutiny ought rather to be directed to my weakness. True reverence lies rather in accepting unmurmuringly the order of things we find; in believing in the completeness and self sufficiency of nature and humanity, and that these contain within them elements of self-sustainment. Our duty is to search there for Truth, to work there patiently for Progress, to regard the humblest conquest there with glad surprise. All virtue is summed up in service and endurance. A wise humility in expectation is surely the first element of reverence. As to the Future Life of man, the whole question lies in a narrow compass. The immortality of the soul is one of those problems which you approach with breathless perplexity. Is it possible that every human being brought into existence, in the caprices of lust and vice, is a candidate for heaven, and a burden upon the celestial taxes, and an inmate of the great Poor House or Reformatory of eternity? Is it in the power of ignorance, profligacy, and passion, to crowd the porticoes of Paradise with illicit offspring? Can it be true that every being born is liable to eternal perdition for acts done before it had existence—or for offences it was predestined to commit, or in the course of events may commit? It is better never to be born than to incur this frightful risk. Is it worth while to live at all the prey of these awful anxieties, to sport for a few years on the borders of Hell? Who would enter the dance of life with the devil for a partner? The toad that croaks his hideous existence away in the marsh; the very dog whom men caress, and kick, and despise; the slimy worm that crawls the grave yard, leads a life of dignity and undimmed bliss, compared with the dread responsibilities and never-ending horrors thus imposed on human consciousness. No man will persuade me that God would bring into existence any creature liable to so frightful a fate. The belief in annihilation is a creed of holiness, in comparison with the creed of the popular religion. If, on the other hand, the future life include no hopeless horror, but a state of purification, of restoration, of atonement, of instruction and progress, however arduous, protracted, and slow, I am willing to believe in it, to hope in it, and rejoice in it. I ask no golden crown—I covet no angel wings—I crave no presumptuous seat of honour at the right hand of God. I supplicate for no effeminate security—no eternity of indolence and singing—I am prepared for toil as well as enjoyment. The instinct of adventure is strong within me. Study and danger are welcome to me—even suffering, if it bring deeper knowledge, purity and improvement. I do not wish to be a 'Saint made perfect,' lingering through an eternity of monotony, in which there is nothing further to realise, but desire rather to enter upon the eternal discipline of indefinite progress. There never were disbelievers in a tolerable immortality. The question is not—is such a state desirable? but—is it true? The vital inquiry is—are we to conduct life on the basis of what we hope or what we know? He who believes in what he wishes, and is willing to teach as true what he desires, has already passed through the gates of superstition.

To honour the brave, to reverence the good, to give thanks to the martyr, to be re-united to those you have loved and lost; if these be the incidents of immortality, there never was a disbeliever in it. The Cosmist only deplores the scantiness of the proof. There is no scepticism here which is wilful. Every doubt is reluctant, every misgiving is a self-denial.

The popular theology, it must be owned, has many repulsive aspects. The vulgarest and most illiterate believer is encouraged to profess a familiar and confident knowledge, hidden from the profoundest philosophers. It is an unanswerable position, that had God spoken, the universe would have been convinced. Had Deity desired that his personal existence should be daily recognised and eternally bruited abroad among men, he would have placarded the fact on the walls of nature in letters of light—so luminous, that time should never pale them; so indelibly, that the war of elements should never efface them; so plainly and conclusively, that no priest should ever be able to misconstrue them; and no wayfarer, in this hurrying world, ever be in doubt about them. As this is not so, the great secret is left evidently to silent thought and reverent conjecture, of which even mere negative Atheism is a reserved expression, and Cosmism a scheme of philosophical adoration.

Here is a particle of matter. It may be amber, or a ruby, or a stone. Whence came the electrical properties of the one, the lurid brilliancy of the other, or the density of the stone? These qualities are wonders and miracles through all time. Science finds them marvels and leaves them mysteries. The philosopher is no more provided with a solution than the peasant. Indeed, the wonder of the philosopher has a deeper intensity. He sweeps with his eye, and bends his ear over a wider field of nature, and no sign rewards his scrutiny, no response repays his attention. Look at this humble, secure, and commonplace stone! We neglect it with the eye, we spurn it with the foot—it is not worth raising from the shore. Yet no book was ever written, no message was ever delivered, no romance ever depicted, no epic ever sung, containing such wondrous interest as the story of this stone, could any man tell it. What thronging conjectures! what unbidden and tumultuous memories rise as we contemplate its possible mutations of existence! History was unwritten when it first slept in the earth. What generations of men have lived and struggled, and died since it was first broken from the rock! Great battles, changing the fate of dynasties, and involving the servitude of races, have been fought over its calm resting place. Possibly thousands of years ago the mastodon trod upon it, and the ichthyosaurus paddled it into the sea. Ancient waves may have washed it into the ocean, before the first ship was launched by the first mariner. In the silent and wondrous caverns of the great deep, which no plummet has fathomed and no eye has ever seen, it has lain in regal rest. What monsters have glared at it! what tempests have raged, what tornadoes have broken over it! what earthquakes may have tossed it up from its hiding place. On what shore did it reappear? Did some Assyrian lover watch the wave which washed it up? Did some young Pharaoh play with it? Has it been imbedded in the walls of Troy? Did Achilles plant his spear by it? Did it lie on the plains of Marathon on the morning of the memorable battle? Has it been dyed by the blood of Caesar in the streets of Rome? Have Chaldean shepherds picked it up as the orient morning sun broke over their silent plains?

When all these and a thousand other questions have been answered, its history is not begun. Its elements are indestructible. The parts of which it is composed were never created—in some form, in some world, they always existed. Where were they when the earth was without form or void? To what astral system did the matter of this pebble once belong? Of what star did it form a part? Where was it before time on this planet began to be? If matter has existed for ever, this stone in its countless transmutations is a geological Wandering Jew of eternity. If we cannot tell the history of a single stone, who shall tell the history of God? If a poor pebble be a surpassing mystery, who shall understand the Deity? What must be the pretension, the presumption to infinite capacity of that man who, pausing not in reverent humility in the presence of these myriad miracles which crowd before him, yet tells us in confident and dogmatic tones, that he

'Looks through Nature up to Nature's God?'

For myself, I cleave rather to that more modest form of opinion which stands in mute wonder and listens with greedy ears to the secret tale of Nature, and waits with undying interest the revelations which science, or thought, or time, or death, shall make of these mysteries which surround us evermore.

CPSIA information can be obtained
at www.ICGtesting.com
Printed in the USA
LVHW041023020323
740706LV00008B/1152

9 789356 891579